Marble Bust of Madame de Sérilly : signed "HOUDON F. 1782."
In the Wallace Collection, London.

Frontispiece.]

VICTORIA AND ALBERT MUSEUM

DEPARTMENT OF WOODWORK

THE PANELLED ROOMS

III. THE BOUDOIR OF MADAME DE SÉRILLY

LONDON: PUBLISHED UNDER THE AUTHORITY
OF THE BOARD OF EDUCATION 1925

Publication No. 109 W.

Crown Copyright Reserved.

First printed 1915.

Reprinted 1925.

This Monograph may be obtained directly from the Victoria and Albert Museum, price 1*s.* 6*d. net* (*by post* 1*s.* 8½*d.*). *It may also be obtained directly from H M. Stationery Office at the following addresses : Adastral House, Kingsway, London, W.C.*2 ; 28, *Abingdon Street, London, S.W.*1; *York Street, Manchester ;* 1, *St. Andrew's Crescent, Cardiff ; or* 120, *George Street, Edinburgh ; or through any bookseller.*

(16573) Wt. P1996/1364 2,000 2/25 Harrow G.45

PREFATORY NOTE

THE thanks of the Board of Education are due to the Trustees of the Wallace Collection for the permission which they have courteously given for the reproduction of the bust of Madame de Sérilly in that collection.

The original design for one side of the room by Rousseau de la Rottière, figured in Plate I, has been reproduced from the "Portefeuille des arts décoratifs, publié sous le patronage de l'Union Centrale des arts décoratifs, par A. de Champeaux," Paris, 1889–1890.

CECIL SMITH.

Victoria and Albert Museum,
August 1915.

NOTE TO SECOND EDITION

Since the first issue of this publication, Madame la Contesse H. de Choiseuil, of Paris, has kindly furnished certain details of personal history relating to Madame de Sérilly, which have justified a slight revision of the text.

ERIC MACLAGAN.

Victoria and Albert Museum,
February 1925.

INTRODUCTORY NOTE

THE painted and gilt room, known as the Boudoir of Madame de Sérilly, removed from a house in the Rue Vieille-du-Temple, Paris, was purchased for the Museum in 1869, and has been re-erected in Room 58 on the ground floor of the Museum (No. 1736-1869). On account both of its historical associations and artistic qualities it must be regarded as one of the most important works of art in the nation's possession.

The following history of the room has been compiled and the description written by Mr. Oliver Brackett, Deputy-Keeper of the Department of Woodwork. The authorities consulted are referred to in the Bibliography. Special mention should be made of the account of the Boudoir by Lady Dilke in " French furniture and decoration of the XVIIIth century." The measured drawings, which, it is hoped, will add to the practical utility of the present publication, have been made by Mr. A. E. Bullock, A.R.I.B.A.

I have read through the proof-sheets.

EDWARD F. STRANGE,
Keeper of Woodwork.

CONTENTS

		PAGE
LIST OF ILLUSTRATIONS	.. ..	8
HISTORY	.. ..	9
DESCRIPTION OF THE ROOM	.. ..	15
LIST OF PHOTOGRAPHS	.. ..	24
BIBLIOGRAPHY	.. ..	25

LIST OF ILLUSTRATIONS

Frontispiece.—Marble Bust of Madame de Sérilly.

PLATE   I.—Original Drawing for one Side of the Room.

„   II.—The Chimney-piece End of the Room.

„   III.—An Angle of the Room.

„   IV.—An Angle of the Room with two Windows.

„   V.—Measured Drawing of Door and Panelling.

„   VI.—The Ceiling.

„   VII.—Measured Drawing of the Ceiling.

„   VIII.—The Chimney-piece.

„   IX.—Two of the Lunettes—Pomona and Neptune.

„   X.—Two of the Lunettes—Vulcan and Juno.

„   XI.—Measured Drawings of Details.

In the text, p. 15.—Plan of the Room.

THE BOUDOIR OF MADAME DE SÉRILLY

HISTORY

IN order to understand the Boudoir of Madame de Sérilly, to appreciate its remarkable qualities and the character of its decoration, it is necessary to consider the state of society at the Court of Louis XVI during the years preceding the Revolution. The storm, soon to burst with such violence, had not yet darkened the horizon, and light clouds passing from time to time were hardly heeded by the fashionable world of Paris, to whom the pursuit of pleasure was the most serious business of life. The old nobility, though still holding a position at the Court, were being, little by little, eclipsed by a younger and more restless society, susceptible to all the new movements—even the cult of Liberty—which were beginning to agitate Europe. "La jeune cour," writes M. Maugras, "pretend innover et surtout mener gaiement l'existence; le plaisir est son unique but; elle le recherche et s'y livre avec une sorte d'ivresse. Ce ne sont que jeux, bals, repetitions, chasses, concerts, fetes de tous genres."[1] The King, by nature retiring, avoided, as far as possible, this unending pursuit of novelty and excitement ; but Marie-Antoinette followed with youthful enthusiasm all the varied fashions, frivolous and intellectual, of the complex and versatile company by which she was surrounded. Side by side with a passion for horse-racing, gambling, masked balls, and scandalous intrigues, there existed a taste for philosophy, for literature—the letters of the time written by both men and women are accomplished literary compositions—and for

[1] "Le duc de Lauzun et la cour de Marie-Antoinette," by A. Maugras. 1895.

painting, sculpture, furniture and the minor arts. Keen rivalry existed to secure the services of well-known artists to paint a portrait, carve a bust, or decorate a room. In spite of the financial crisis which was threatening the country, in spite of rumours of war and popular discontent, reckless extravagance reigned at the Court, carried to such a pitch that between 1780 and 1790 famous families went bankrupt in their endeavour to keep pace with the expensive habits of the time. This tendency conspicuous in dress, entertainment and the like, was no less visible in decoration and furniture. In spite, however, of the extravagance of the age, artists of the period preserved a high standard of artistic restraint combined with an almost over-sensitive appreciation of classical accuracy in form and technical efficiency in execution. All these conflicting qualities are reflected in the Boudoir of Madame de Sérilly.

In 1869 when the Boudoir was purchased for the Museum, a story was attached to it which in course of time has come to be regarded as history. According to this account, M. de Sérilly, an army paymaster under Louis XVI, living in the Rue St. Louis, married one of the favourite maids-of-honour of Queen Marie-Antoinette. During his absence from Paris his wife, with the assistance of the Queen, caused this Boudoir to be fitted up as a surprise for him on his return. Except that the Hotel Sérilly was situated in the Rue Vieille-du-Temple and not in the Rue St. Louis, the main features of the story are borne out by subsequent investigation. History corroborates the general statements about M. and Madame de Sérilly, though the surprise of the Boudoir may be merely a touch of sentiment. The ceiling of the room bears representations of the eagle, as a compliment, no doubt, to Marie-Antoinette, and the bulk of the ornamentation was carried out by Rousseau de la Rottière, whose talents the Queen almost exclusively monopolised and who was engaged about this time in decorating the private apartments at Versailles and Fontainebleau.

8

MÉGRET DE SÉRILLY AND HIS WIFE.

Antoine-Jean-François Mégret de Sérilly. born on 14th September 1746, belonged to an historic family of which the records date back to the 14th century. He held by inheritance the post of "Trésorier général de l'extraordinaire des guerres" receiving the additional honour of "Maître des requêtes" in 1779.[1] The arms of the family bore the coronet of a marquis, which title seems sometimes to have been given unofficially to Mégret de Sérilly. In 1779 he married his cousin Anne-Marie-Louise Thomas de Pange de Domangeville, an interval of seventeen years separating their ages. From the date of the marriage it can be assumed that the Boudoir was executed about 1780 or shortly afterwards. The portrait bust in the Wallace Collection (see frontispiece) shows Madame de Sérilly in her nineteenth year.[2] There seems no corroboration of the statement that Madame de Sérilly was a lady-of-honour to Marie-Antoinette. In fact both Mégret de Sérilly and his wife are best known to history through their fatal friendship with the sister of Louis XVI, Madame Elisabeth of France, whose amiable character presents a somewhat marked contrast to that of some of her contemporaries. They carried on a correspondence with Madame Elisabeth during the Revolution, and their names, as well as that of Mégret d'Etigny, the brother of Sérilly, occur on the list of twenty-four persons accused of being agents and accomplices with the princess in an alleged plot to assist Louis XVI,

[1] See " Annuaire de la Noblesse de France," by A. Borel d'Hauterive. Vol. 45. 1889. A most interesting account of the Sérilly family, based partly on information obtained from private sources, is given by Lady Dilke in " French furniture and decoration of the XVIIIth century," but contains statements which disagree on certain points with Borel d'Hauterive and other authorities.

[2] Signed : " Houdon F. 1872." Exhibited at the Salon 1783. Bought about 1864 by a Paris dealer at a sale of Sérilly effects at Theil (Yonne). Purchased afterwards by the duc de Morny, and figured at his sale 31 May 1865. (See " Dictionnaire des sculpteurs de l'école française," by S. Lami, 1911).

a charge on which they were eventually condemned to death by the Revolutionary Tribunal. The entries on the official report (*procès-verbal d'exécution*) are interesting :—" 15. Antoine-Jean-François Mégret de Sérilly, ci-devant trésorier-général de la guerre, et depuis cultivateur, agé de quarante-huit ans, natif de Paris, domicilié à Passy, près Sens." "23. Anne-Marie Louise Thomas, agée de trente et un ans, native de Paris, domiciliée a Passy, département de l'Yonne, mariée a Mégret Sérilly."[1] Thus it seems that during these stormy years Mégret de Sérilly with his wife had left the house in the Rue Vieille-du-Temple for the more peaceful neighbourhood of Passy, where the former was devoting himself to farming. The most definite charge brought against Madame Elisabeth was that of obtaining possession of the State diamonds, the property of the nation, which she was accused of handing over to her brother, the Comte d'Artois, in order to aid Louis to raise an army " pour assassiner le peuple, anéantir la liberté et rétablir le despotisme." Although the charges were denied, Madame Elisabeth was executed on the 27th May 1794, as well as the other victims implicated, with the exception of Madame de Sérilly, whose sentence of death was altered to imprisonment on the strength of a declaration that she was about to become a mother.[2] In the following year at the trial of Fouquier-Tinville, the public prosecutor, who was accused of sanctioning the execution of women in these circumstances, Madame de Sérilly was called as a witness, a curious point arising from the discovery that her name and place of execution had been inserted on the death register.[3] In his defence Fouquier-Tinville stated that this was a notorious device for escaping the

[1] A copy of this document is attached to " Correspondance de Madame Elisabeth," by F. Feuillet de Conches. 1868.
[2] " Le même jour, entre quatre et cinq heures du soir tous les ci-dessus denommés ont été conduits sur la place de la Revolution, à l'exception de la femme Sérilly qui s'est declarée enceinte, et qui a obtenu un sursis." (" *Procès d'Elisabeth-Marie Capet, sœur de Louis XVI.*")
[3] *See* " Le Tribunal Révolutionnaire," by G. Lenôtre. 1908.

scaffold.[1] The report, generally accepted, that the declaration
was false in the case of Madame de Sérilly is probably correct,
since her fourth and youngest child was born about four years
before her trial.[2] According to the Diary of Pierre Danloux,
Madame de Sérilly, in 1796, was married for the second time to
her kinsman, the Chevalier de Pange.[3]

The Hôtel Sérilly.

The house in which the Boudoir was constructed was formerly
No. 122 (now 106), Rue Vieille-du-Temple, in the district of
the Temple, Paris. In the late 18th century this neighbourhood
was full of great houses, many of which remain to-day, though
the district is now a thickly-populated business quarter. According
to tradition, the architect of the Boudoir was Claude-Nicholas
Ledoux (b. 1736 ; d. 1806). There is no reason for doubting
this attribution, since Ledoux was responsible for several fashionable pavilions of this type ; but it is doubtful if he had anything
further to do with the building which, from descriptions by both
M. de Champeaux [4] and M. Contet,[5] must have been an imposing
mansion dating back to the 17th century. A plan of the Hôtel
Sérilly, given to the Museum in 1869 by Madame Achille Jubinal,
shows the house facing the Rue Vieille-du-Temple, with a garden
behind stretching to the Rue St. Gervais.[6] This is a lithograph
plan of about 1850, but that the relative position of the two
streets was the same in the 18th century is shown by a map
attached to the official description of Paris, published in 1714,[7]
the house being at that date described as Hôtel d'Epernon. In the
first half of the 18th century the Hôtel d'Epernon belonged to the

1 " Réponse d'Antoine-Quentin Fouquier, ex-accusateur-public au différens
chefs d'accusation."
2 *See* Borel d'Hauterive (as above).
3 " Pierre Danloux et son journal," by Baron R. Portalis.
4 " L'art décoratif dans le vieux Paris," by A. de Champeaux. 1898.
5 " Les vieux hôtels de Paris," by F. Contet. 1910.
6 The plan is exhibited with the Boudoir in the Museum.
7 " Description de la ville et les Faubourgs de Paris."

family of Mauregard, but after a lawsuit passed into the possession of the Marquis de Pange who, in 1776, sold it to Mégret de Sérilly for 180,000 livres. The plan given by Madame Jubinal is executed in minute detail and possesses great interest, not only since it definitely determines the situation of the house, but because it enables the mind to reconstruct the arrangement of the building and the grounds, and to imagine to some extent the romantic outlook on which the windows of the Boudoir opened. Entered from the Rue Vieille-du-Temple, the house formed an irregular square surrounding a courtyard, the farther side opening on to a garden, which, bounded by a wall on each side, stretched as far as the Rue St. Gervais. The garden was methodically laid out with lawns, pools of water, and pavilions after the fashion of the time. The principal pavilion, with paintings by Boucher, stood in the centre of the grounds beyond the pools. In one of the angles formed by the back of the house and the boundary wall the Boudoir was placed, its windows facing the garden. In such a position it could easily have been added by Ledoux without affecting the main structure.

After the tragedy which overtook the Sérilly family at the end of the century, the property was confiscated by the Revolutionary Government and put up for auction. After various vicissitudes it came in 1846 into the possession of a certain M. de St. Albin, passing, afterwards, to his daughter, Madame Achille Jubinal. In 1867 the Boudoir was acquired and removed by M. Recappé, from whom, two years later, it was purchased for the Museum.[1] Other panelling in the house has since been sold to an American, and nothing of the original interior decoration now remains except a few panels and carvings. No information is at present forthcoming as to the fate of the pavilion painted by Boucher. The house and courtyard are still standing, though used for business purposes.

[1] The statement that the Hôtel Sérilly was situated in the Rue St. Louis was current at this date. It was afterwards accepted by Lady Dilke. As a matter of fact, the Rue St. Louis did not touch the house nor the garden. The description of the house given by M. Contet in " Les vieux hôtels de Paris " (1910) removes all doubt as to its position and history.

DESCRIPTION OF ROOM

GENERAL.

The dimensions of the room are as follows :—

Height, 16 ft.
Length, 14 ft.
Width, 10 ft. 6 in.

The scheme of arrangement consists of four lofty walls built on a square plan with two projecting bays and surmounted by a

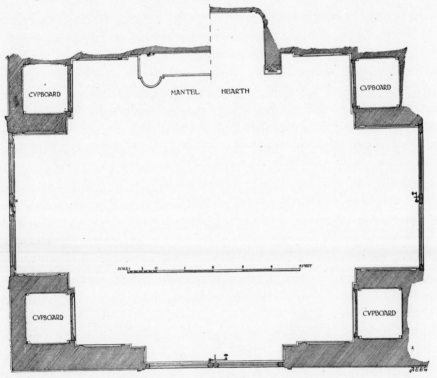

Plan of the Room.

coved ceiling. Each wall is composed of an arch flanked by two tall panels or pilasters with smaller panels below the dado-rail ; the arches enclose the chimney-piece, door and two windows, and project outwards, in the case of the side walls, to form shallow

13

bays ;[1] behind the panelling in each angle are two cupboards with hinged panels to form doors, the larger cupboard above the dado-rail being fitted with serrated uprights to support bookshelves. All the surface is decorated with ornament partly in relief, painted in various colours and embellished with gilding.

THE WALL DECORATION :

Jean-Simon Rousseau de la Rottière [b. 1747].

The eight long panels of the walls flanking the central arches are decorated with compositions symbolical of the Four Seasons, arranged in pairs. The same general scheme of ornament is adopted throughout. The motive of each panel consists of a figure holding a festoon and supporting a basket of flowers, from which issue conventional scrolls and flowering sprays, cunningly interwoven, in each panel, with a candelabrum and candlesticks ; three medallions painted with figure and animal compositions are distributed over the surface at regular intervals (Plates II, III, IV). Slight variations of detail occur according to the season depicted. Thus the two figures typifying Spring are youthful and winged ; those representing Summer have suitable attributes ; the pair devoted to Autumn are shown as figures of Bacchus crowned with the vine ; and Winter is symbolised by two sombre old women, each bearing a chain. This dominant idea runs all through the decorative scheme of the panels. Roses, wheat, vine, and laurel are introduced for different times of year as well as such devices as anchors (hope), scythes, wine-cups and skates. The bulk of the ornament is executed in composition, coloured and gilt, but, in order to give relief, certain features are painted direct on the wood. The standing figures are represented in imitation of bronze ; vivid and realistic colours express the flowers and fruit ; red and blue form the ground of the medallions. The rest of the ornament

[1] For constructional reasons the door replaces one of the windows in the position in which the room has been erected in the Museum.

14

and the mouldings are gilt. All this variety of colour is harmonized by the background of pale yellowish-grey, an indefinable tint to which Time has added an element of subtlety.

Within the arches of the side wall the surface is painted with classical figures in panels and a variety of ornamental devices intended to symbolise Love and the Chase. None of the latter decoration is executed in relief.

In 1869, when the Boudoir was purchased for the Museum, the painted decoration was erroneously ascribed to Fragonard and Natoire. Some years later, however, the fortunate discovery of an original design by Rousseau de la Rottière for one of the walls disposed of the doubtful attributions which had hitherto been current. This design, one of a collection of drawings by Rousseau, belonging to his grandson M. Gillet, was reproduced in the "Portefeuille des arts décoratifs" for 1889–1890. It is an outline drawing and a document of great value, showing that Rousseau's original conception was faithfully carried out except in the matter of a few details. In the drawing a fanlight replaces the lunette painting above the window, and the elaborate ornament of the ceiling, as executed, is not suggested (Plate I).

Jean-Simon Rousseau de la Rottière belonged to a family which for a hundred years or more had been engaged on the decoration of public buildings in France. His father, Jules-Antoine Rousseau, was particularly famous for ornamental sculpture accomplished under these circumstances. The National Archives of France show that between 1740 and 1788 Jules-Antoine was almost continuously employed at the Palace of Versailles, and during the same period at Fontainebleau, at the chateaux of Chambord, Choisy, Compiègne, and St. Hubert, the principle royal residences to which Louis XV and his Court had been in the habit of paying an annual visit, progressing from house to house as the year advanced. His labours were well rewarded, for it is no uncommon thing to find that in one year he received 20,000 to 30,000 livres in payment. But his debts were often unpaid, and by 1790 he was owed 121,500 livres for work executed at Versailles. His two sons, Jules-Hugues and Jean-Simon (Rousseau de la Rottière), worked with him and carried on the traditions of the family.[1] Information is scanty about Jules-Hugues, who is supposed, like his father, to have devoted himself to sculpture ; but a definite outline of the career of his brother, the decorator of the Boudoir, can be sketched from records available. He was born in 1747, and at an early age assumed the surname " de la Rottière." As a young man he distinguished himself as a student at the Acadèmie Royale. When about twenty years of age he began to assist his father on the commissions which the latter was undertaking. The drawings which M. Gillet possesses are dated between 1780 and 1789, and show that Rousseau de la Rottière was responsible for work at Versailles, in the private apartments of the King, the Queen, and Madame Adelaide, the King's aunt. He is also supposed to have decorated the Bedroom of Marie-Antoinette at Fontainebleau. He specialized essentially in the Pompeian style of decoration. The discoveries at Herculaneum and Pompeii about the middle of the 18th century offered novel schemes of ornament which a capricious public eagerly adopted and grafted on to their native style. Though possessing a somewhat trivial imagination, Rousseau de la Rottière was unquestionably a master of his art, and both his drawings and paintings suggest that he worked with that facility which is a mark, if not of genius, at least of talent. The characteristics of his style and his relative importance as an artist have

[1] The main statements as to the relationship of the Rousseau family quoted above are taken from " Dictionnaire des sculpteurs de l'école française," by S. Lami (1911). M. de Champeaux, in " La peinture décorative " (1890), names the elder brother Antoine, apparently confusing the father with the son. Lami's Dictionary, however, was published more than ten years later than De Champeaux's book, and as most of the information contained in it is taken from the National Archives, it can be regarded as the most modern and reliable authority. Lady Dilke also gives a valuable account of the career of Rousseau de la Rottière.

been summed up, though with perhaps unduly critical severity, by M. Molinier, the well-known historian of French art: "Jean Simeon Rousseau de la Rottière est un continuateur des décorateurs de Pompéi et un successeur inconscient des fabricants de grotesques du XVI° siecle en Italie. Il puise aux mêmes sources, mais, comme sa veine est courte, qu'il a juste l'intelligence de l'antiquité et l'imagination d'un miniaturiste tel que De Gault, il se tire, par la symétrie, de tous les motifs de décoration qu'il imagine et déguise sa pauvreté en appliquant ses peintures sur des fonds satinés ou argentés, chatoyants, agréables, à l'œil et se mariant à merveille avec les soieries des ameublements. Mais, au fond, c'est un pauvre artiste, un indigent, quand on le compare aux décorateurs du règne de Louis XV. Toutes ces reflexions faites, les ensembles qu'il a peints sont parfois charmants, et constituent en tout cas un document important dans l'histoire de l'évolution du style français dans la seconde moitié du XVIII° siècle." [1]

THE CEILING.

The ceiling is of coved section and decorated with a circular painting of Jupiter in the clouds, surrounded by borders painted and gilt (Plate VI). The ornament is modelled in higher relief than that of the walls, and the colours are deeper in tone. Thus the demi-figures of cupids in the borders are bronzed, and the scrolls gilt all on a deep blue marbled ground; bronze colour, also, is used for the shells in the angles, and red for the ground of the small medallions; the rest of the ornament and the mouldings are gilt and silvered   It has been conjectured that the eagles in the spandrels outside the central panel were intended as a compliment to Marie-Antoinette, who was the daughter of the Emperor Francis I, though, if strict heraldry were followed, the imperial eagle should be two-headed. This device of an

[1] " Le mobilier royal français," by E. Molinier. 1902.

eagle was not uncommon on French buildings of the time of Louis XVI ; it occurs on a ceiling in the Hôtel de Monnaies, built by Antoine, and is found (but without the wreath) in the decoration of the walls of the "Salon des Jeux" of Marie-Antoinette, at Fontainebleau. Whether the decoration of the ceiling of the Boudoir was carried out by Rousseau de la Rottière is unknown. His drawing shows only a square panel as ornament for this part of the room ; but it is not improbable that his father or brother were responsible for the work, since it is mainly of a sculpturesque nature.

THE OIL PAINTINGS ON THE WALLS AND CEILING :

Jean Jacques Lagrenée le jeune [*b.* 1740 ; *d.* 1821].

The lunettes within the arches of the walls are painted in oil colours on canvas with mythological figures symbolical of the elements, Earth, Air, Fire and Water. Earth is represented by Pomona, a comely girl, with attributes of Plenty ; Juno with peacocks typifies Air ; Vulcan with forge and hammer illustrates Fire ; and Neptune is depicted as the symbol of Water (Plates IX and X). The circular panel on the ceiling is similarly painted with Jupiter astride an eagle in the clouds. Athough no documentary evidence seems, up to the present, to be forthcoming, these paintings have been attributed—and the attribution is generally accepted—to Lagrenée le jeune, a prolific artist who, between 1760 and 1804, executed numerous paintings of classical, mythological and sacred subjects. The Boudoir paintings cannot be traced in the list of works of Lagrenée which M. Bellier de la Chavignerie[1] has arranged in chronological sequence ; but, the

[1] "Dictionnaire général des artistes de l'école française," by E. Bellier de la Chavignerie. 1882.

18

year 1781 contains the entry " Esquisses du plafond et des quatres dessins de porte du salon de M. Saint-James," showing that at the date of the construction of the Boudoir, Lagrenée was engaged on painting of this character.

THE CHIMNEY-PIECE.

Claude Michel, called Clodion [*b.* 1738 ; *d.* 1814].

Pierre Gouthière [*b. about* 1740].

The chimney-piece is of grey marble with white marble terminals, sculptured with figures of bearded men, applied to the jambs ; elaborate gilt bronze mounts enrich the frieze and the terminals (Plate VIII). The shelf is fashioned with rounded projected ends intended to support candelabra with branching lights such as, in conjunction with a central clock and intermediate vases, formed the customary adornment of mantel-shelves at the time of Louis XVI. The terminal figures, of which the execution is in every respect masterly, have been attributed to Clodion ; they are quoted by M. Lami in a comprehensive list of this sculptor's works.[1] Pierre Gouthière, the famous metal-worker, is said to have executed the mountings of the chimney-piece. It has been the custom for many years to assign to Gouthière such metal mounts of the time of Louis XVI as are of exceptionally fine quality, but, more often than not, no authority except tradition exists for such attributions. Although described on signed pieces as " cizeleur et doreur du roy," the name of Gouthière is not found in the National Accounts between 1773 and 1786, during which period he seems to have been mainly employed by Madame du Barry and the Duc d'Aumont. The mounts on the Boudoir chimney-piece, however, bear a considerable resemblance to mounts on furniture definitely assigned to Gouthière, so that there are good reasons for assuming that he may have been the metal-worker employed.

[1] " Dictionnaire des sculpteurs de l'école française," by S. Lami. 1911.

Compare, for instance, the authenticated gilt bronze mounts on a porphyry table in the collection of the Duc d'Aumont, and illustrated in the catalogue of his sale held in Paris on 12th December 1782.

The grate of the chimney-piece is lined with three firebacks of cast iron decorated with figures and ornament showing a Chinese influence and presumably somewhat earlier in date than the rest of the room.

The overmantel consists of a rectangular mirror in gilt frame. A water-colour drawing of the Boudoir, probably executed before its demolition, shows gilt festoons suspended in front of the mirror —a device not uncommon at the time of Louis XVI. Unless, therefore, this was merely a licence taken by the artist for picturesque reasons, it seems probable the original mirror was broken before the room came into the possession of the Museum.

THE WHOLE COMPOSITION.

Without a doubt the men engaged on the work were the best to be obtained, but the employment of such a galaxy of talent on one small room might have proved a failure if the architect had not possessed the power of blending the varied elements of decoration into one harmonious whole. Ledoux was obviously gifted with this faculty. There is not a jarring note in the composition, The construction, on so small a plan, of a room destined to receive such a wealth of ornamentation must have presented great difficulties. The excessive height, however, does not strike the spectator as disproportionate. Monotony is avoided by the projecting bays on each side, which break the regularity of plan ; the appreciation of values is shown by the contrast between the low relief ornament of the panels and the bolder modelling on the ceiling, just as the faint hues and subtle colouring of the walls stand out against the deeper tones visible as the eye travels upwards. Again, the technique, even the joinery, is carried out with that masterly precision and perfect finish which was characteristic of the French artists of the 18th century. From such points of view the room presents an object lesson to architects, students, and craftsmen. That under modern conditions of life it would prove a successful model for reproduction is improbable. Such a lavish display of ornament would weary the eye if applied to a room of normal proportions ; and such an atmosphere of luxurious refinement would be unsuited to an age of more serious ambitions and to a nation of more severe, though less brilliant, qualities.

OLIVER BRACKETT.

PHOTOGRAPHS

The following photographs are in the Museum Collection, and can be seen on application in the Library. Prints from the official negatives may be purchased at the Photograph Stall in the Museum. The numbers in parentheses are those of the official negatives :—

> Angle, with portion of chimney-piece and window (right) (18194, 18195).
> Angle, with portion of chimney-piece and door (left) (18196, 38612).
> Angle, with two windows (38613).
> Ceiling (17917, 38614).
> Chimney-piece (marble) (38616).
> Details (17918, 17919, 18197).
> Paintings (lunettes) (38607, 38608, 38609, 38610).
> Wall, end, with chimney-piece and portion of panelling (18198, 38615).

The following drawings are exhibited with the Boudoir in the Museum :—

> Water-colour drawing of the room. [Acquired at the same date as the room.] Photo. Neg. No. 13152.
> Plan of Hôtel Sérilly [lith. Lemercier], given by Madame Achille Jubinal.

BIBLIOGRAPHY

BELLIER DE LA CHAVIGNERIE, E.—Dictionnaire général des artistes de l'école française. Paris, 1882.

BIOGRAPHIE UNIVERSELLE.

BOREL D'HAUTERIVE, A.—Annuaire de la Noblesse de France. Vol. XLV. 1889. [Biography of Sérilly family.]

BRICE, Germain.—Description da la ville de Paris. Paris, 1752.

CHAMPEAUX, A. DE.—Portefeuille des arts décoratifs. Vols. II. and III. Paris, 1889–91. [Reproductions of drawings by Rousseau de la Rottière.]

CHAMPEAUX, A. DE.—L'art décoratif dans le vieux Paris. Paris, 1898. [Description of Hôtel Sérilly.]

CHAMPEAUX, A. DE.—Histoire de la peinture décorative. Paris, 1890. [Notes on Rousseau de la Rottière.]

CHANDENIER, Felix.—Madame de Sérilly échappée à l'échaufaud sous la Terreur (*Bulletin de la Société Archéologique de Sens*, 1894).

CONTET, F.—Les vieux hôtels de Paris. Vol. I. Paris, 1910. [Description of Hôtel Sérilly, with illustrations of Boudoir.]

DALY, C.—Motifs historiques ; décorations intérieures. Vol. II. Paris (1880). [Engraved plates : No. 51, Portion of Ceiling ; No. 52, Chimney-piece.]

D'AUMONT, M. le Duc.—Catalogue des effets précieux qui composent le Cabinet du feu M. le Duc d'Aumont. (Sale : Paris, 12 Dec. 1782.) [Authentic works by Gouthière.]

DESTAILLEUR, René.—Documents de décoration au XVIIIe siècle. Paris, 1906. [Rousseau de la Rottière.]

DILKE, E. F. S., *Lady*.—Le Boudoir de la Marquise de Sérilly. (In Gazette des Beaux-Arts, XX. 1898.)

DILKE, E. F. S., *Lady*.—French Furniture and Decoration in the 18th century. London, 1901.

ELIZABETH PHILIPPINA MARIA HELEN, *Princess of France.*—Procès d'Elisabeth-Marie-Capet, sœur de Louis XVI. 1798.

FEUILLET DE CONCHES, F. S., *Baron.*—Correspondance de Madame Elisabeth. Paris, 1868.

FOUQUIER-TINVILLE, A. Q.—Réponse d'A. Q. Fouquier aux differens chefs d'accusation. 1795. [Remission of sentence on Madame de Sérilly.]

GAZETTE DES BEAUX-ARTS.—*See* Dilke, Lady : Nolhac, P. de.

GUIFFREY, J.—Les Caffieri. Paris, 1877. [Notes on Gouthière.]

HAVARD, H.—Dictionnaire de l'ameublement et de la décoration. Paris. [Boudoir.]

LAMI, STANISLAS.—Dictionnaire des sculpteurs de l'école française. Paris, 1911.

LENÔTRE, G.—Le Tribunal Révolutionnaire. Paris, 1908.

LONDON : WALLACE COLLECTION.—Catalogue.

MAUGRAS, G.—Le duc de Lauzun et la cour de Marie-Antoinette. Paris, 1895.

MOLINIER, Émile.—Le mobilier au XVIIᵉ et au XVIIIᵉ siècle. Paris (1898).

MOLINIER, Émile.—Le mobilier royal français. Paris, 1902. [Criticism of Rousseau de la Rottière.]

NOLHAC, P. DE.—La décoration de Versailles au XVIIIᵉ siècle. [In Gazette des Beaux-Arts, XIX 1898.]

PARIS.—Description de la ville et les faubourgs de Paris. Dressée et gravée sous les ordres de M. D'Argenson, Conseilleur du Roy en son conseil d'Etat, Lieutenant General de la Ville, Prevosté et Vicomté de Paris. 1714. [Map of Paris.]

PFNOR, R —L'architecture, décoration et ameublement : époque Louis XVI. Paris, 1865.

PFNOR, R.—Architecture et décoration au Palais de Fontainebleau. Paris, 1885.

PIGANIOL DE LA FORCE, M.—Description de Paris. Paris, 1742.

PLANAT, P.—Le style Louis XVI. Paris (1907).

PORTALIS, ROGER, *Baron*.—Henry-Pierre Danloux et son journal durant l'Emigration. Paris, 1910. [History of the Sérilly Family.]

RICCI, Seymour de.—Louis XVI Furniture. (Paris 1913). [Interiors at Fontainebleau and Versailles.]

ROBIQUET, Jacques.—Gouthière : sa vie-son œuvre. Paris, 1912.

ROCHEGUDE, *Marquis de*.—Guide pratique à travers le vieux Paris (1903).

ROUSSEL, J.—Le Palais de Fontainebleau. Paris (1899). [Boudoir of Marie Antoinette].

STRANGE, T. A.—French Interiors, Furniture, Decoration, during the 17th and 18th centuries. London. [Illustrations of Sérilly Boudoir.]

NOTICE

THIS Monograph may be obtained directly from the Director and Secretary, Victoria and Albert Museum, London, S.W.7, price 1s. 6d. net (by post 1s. 8½d.). It may also be obtained from H.M. Stationery Office at the following addresses : Adastral House, Kingsway, London, W.C.2; 28, Abingdon Street, London S.W.1 ; York Street, Manchester ; 1, St. Andrew's Crescent, Cardiff ; or 120, George Street, Edinburgh ; or through any Bookseller.

Other publications of the Department of Woodwork are shown below :—

Publication No.   *Catalogues.*

9 w   **Musical Instruments.** By Carl Engel. pp. 402 ; 6 photographs and 143 wood-cuts. Roy. 8vo. 1874. 12s. [By post 12s. 9d.]

154 w   **English Furniture and Woodwork.** Vol. I. Gothic and Early Tudor. By H. Clifford Smith. pp. viii and 68 ; 57 plates. Crown 4to. 1923. 2s. 6d. [By post 2s. 10½d.] Cloth 4s. [By post 4s. 6d.]

149   **The Jones Collection.** Part I. Furniture. By Oliver Brackett. pp. viii and 36 ; 49 plates. Crown 4to. 1922. 2s. 6d. [By post 2s. 10d.] Cloth 3s. 6d. [By post 4s.]

159 w   **Catalogue of Japanese Lacquer.** Part I. General. By Edward F. Strange. pp. viii and 193 ; 49 plates. Crown 4to. 1924. 5s. [By post 5s. 6d.] Cloth 7s. 6d. [By post 8s. 3d.]

160 w   **Catalogue of Japanese Lacquer.** Part II. [*In preparation.*]

161 w   **Catalogue of Chinese Lacquer.** [*In preparation.*]

Monographs on the Panelled Rooms.

104 w   I. **The Bromley Room.** pp. 21 ; 18 plates. Crown 4to. Paper boards. 1922. 1s. 6d. [By post 1s. 8½d.]

105 w   II. **The Clifford's Inn Room.** pp. 16 ; 13 plates. Crown 4to. Paper boards. 1922. 1s. 6d. [By post 1s. 8½d.]

116 w   IV. **The Sizergh Castle Room.** pp. 34 ; 16 plates. Crown 4to. Paper boards. 1915. 6d. [By post 8½d.)

134 w   V. **The Hatton Garden Room.** pp. 19 ; 9 plates. Crown 4to. Paper boards. 1920. 1s. 6d. [By post 1s. 8½d.]

166 w   VI. **The Waltham Abbey Room.** pp. 24 ; 17 plates. Crown 4to. Paper boards 1924. 1s. 6d. By post 1s. 8½d.]

Handbook.

125 w   **The Accounts of Chippendale, Haig and Co.,** for the furnishing of David Garrick's House in the Adelphi. pp. 20 ; 1 plate. Roy. 8vo. 1920. 2s. [By post 2s. 1d.]

For the portfolios of reproductions of **Measured Drawings of French Furniture,** published by Mr. W. G. Paulson Townsend, and for the plates of **French Wood Carvings,** published by Messers.. B. T. Batsford, Ltd., *see* List 2a.

Orders should be accompanied by a remittance, including postage.

PLATE I.

Original design for one side of the Room : by Rousseau de la Rottière.
Reproduced from " Portefeuille des arts décoratifs."

PLATE II.

The chimney-piece end of the Room.

Wall decoration by Rousseau de la Rottière : lunette attributed to Lagrenée
le jeune ; chimney-piece attributed to Clodion and Gouthière.

PLATE III.

An angle of the Room.

PLATE IV.

An angle of the Room with two windows.

PLATE V.

SCALE. FEET

A E Bullock Pub.

Measured drawing of door and panelling.

PLATE VI.

The Ceiling.

PLATE VII.

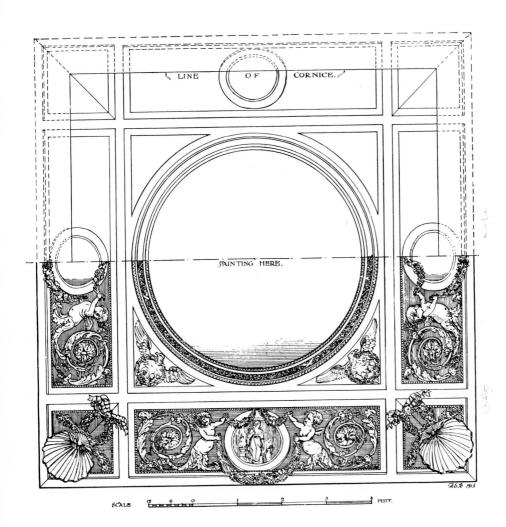

LINE   OF   CORNICE.

PAINTING HERE.

SCALE   12   6   0   1   2   3   4   FEET.

Measured drawing of the ceiling.

PLATE VIII.

Chimney-piece of marble, attributed to Clodion, with gilt bronze mounts attributed to Gouthière.

PLATE IX.

Pomona.

Neptune.

Lunettes painted in oil colours.

PLATE X.

Vulcan.

Juno.

Lunettes painted in oil colours.

PLATE XI.

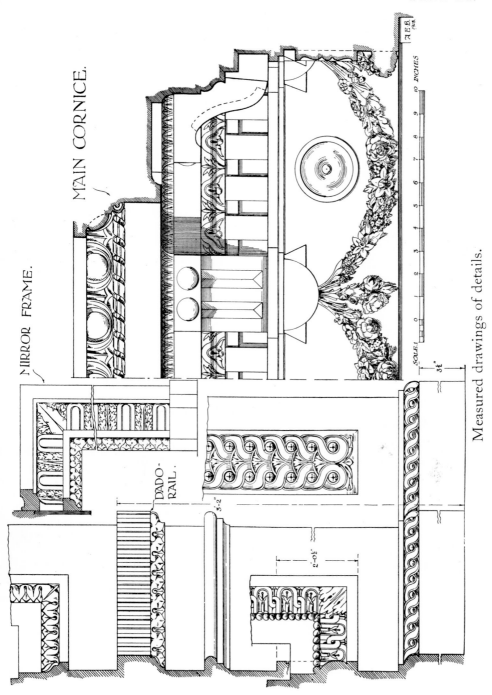

MAIN CORNICE.

MIRROR FRAME.

DADO-RAIL.

Measured drawings of details.